Poems on the Barack Obama Presidency

by Veta E. Wilson

DORRANCE PUBLISHING CO
EST. 1920
PITTSBURGH, PENNSYLVANIA 15238

Dorrance Publishing Co
585 Alpha Drive
Pittsburgh, PA 15238
Visit our website at *www.dorrancebookstore.com*

ISBN: 979-8-8852-7528-6
eISBN: 978-1-6393-7718-3

Poems on the Barack Obama Presidency

Table of Contents

A Haitian Prayer 1

A Mosque Near Ground Zero 2

A Teachable Moment is Lost 3

America 5

Barack Obama Recipient 2009 Nobel Peace Prize 6

Birds 7

Cholera in Haiti 8

Boots 9

Angels 10

Come Quickly 11

Death 12

Dem Ole im 13

Discontent 14

Disgusted with Old Age 16

Egypt 17

Election Results 19

Fear 20

Final Assault 21

Fisherman 22

Forgetfulness 23

Freedom has many Hats 24

Freedom 25

From the Project to the Presidency 26

Goodbye, My Son 28

Haiti After the Earthquake 30

Haiti 31

Haitians Celebrate 32

Hope 33

It's Not My Cup of Tea 34

Joy 35

Longing for Peace 36

Massachusetts 37

Michael Jackson 39

Mid Term Elections 2010 – Part 1 41

Mid Term Elections 2010 – Part 2 42

Oil Spill 43

Playful Pals 45

Quatrain 1 46

Quatrain 2 47

Quietness 48

Realization 49

Reflection – 1 51

Reflection – 2 52

Republicans 53

Shout 54

Sleep 55

Spring 56

Synopsis 57

Terrorism 58

The End of an Era 60

The Hour has Come 62

The President is in Danger 64

The Time Has Come – 1 66

Tragedy at Fort Hood 68

Tsunami 70

Unjust World 72

Osama Bin Laden Is Dead 74

Walk Good 76

Weather Forecast 77

Woman with Child After the Quake 78

Honduras Political Crisis 79

A Brighter Day 80

A Man is a Man 81

Adam Smith, Where Are You? 83

Advice to Kate on Her Wedding Day 84

Bill Clinton 85

First Lady 87
Forty-Seven Percent 88
God's Plan 89
He is an American 90
How to Find Pleasure in Old Age 91
In God's Hands 92
Less We Forget 93
Look to the Future 95
Looking to the Future with Anger 96
Mitt Romney and His Income Tax Returns 97
Mitt Romney 98
My Best Friend 99
On the Beach 100
Presidential Nominee 101
Racism 102
Romney Fest Up 103
The Time Has Come – 2 104
True Love 106
Veta Molly Wilson 107
Victory Night 108
We must not forget 109
Whitney Houston 110
I Am Alpha and Omega 111
I Hear Different Tunes 112
Inauguration Day 113
Inauguration Pledge 115
The Decline of the GOP 117
The Only Women 119
The Presidential Race 120
The Slaughter of the Innocent 121
Backlash from the Tea Party Movement 123
He didn't lie to us knowingly 125
Nelson Mandela 127
Racism a Reluctant Topic 128
The End of My Two Terms 129
A Week of Victories 130

Early Reflection on My Presidency 132
Hilary Clinton for President 133
Political Dog Fight. 134
Violence in the United States of America 135
Wat a Courageous Woman 136
White House Briefing 137

A Haitian Prayer

O Lord, how long will you let these people suffer?
Cholera killed 750 thousand.
Everybody knew that this would happen.
Because of poor sanitation after the Earthquake of January 12th.

All the rivers were polluted.
But those who came to help them turned a blind eye.
Some countries did not honor their pledge.
Because of more natural disasters in other countries.

Friends sometime forsake you, but the struggle for survival continues.
Although it would appear that God has abandoned you.
Do not encourage that thought!
God will never leave you; he is just a prayer away.

Ask God to intervene and get those who
Are behind in their contribution to pay up
And pray that no more disasters come to your country.
God is your anchor in times of trouble.

Wednesday, November 24, 2010

A Mosque Near Ground Zero

What a pity that America wants to
Enfranchise the Muslims!
Do they know what the Koran says about non-Muslims?
They are infidels!
Wait 'till the Americans find out.

The English experience is sad.
They took in many Muslims when Kenya expelled then.
The thanks they got!
Murders in the Underground.
The Streets of Rumford—An Open Market.

England is Sharia compliant!
Mosques all over the country.
What a victory for the Muslims
When they have accomplished their goal!
A mosque near Ground Zero.

Sunday August 29, 2010

A Teachable Moment Is Lost

It is recognized by all that President
Obama does not like to discuss racism.
Many of his problems are as a result of his
Failure to do so.

Shirley Sherrod incident with "The Tea Party" and the NAACP
Furnished an opportunity to explore racism and all its facets
However, once more this opportunity was missed.

President Jimmy Carter said that much of the problems
That President Obama encountered
And continues to encounter are due to racism.
President Carter was criticized by the media.

President Carter's observation is a valid one.
Because he was born and raised in the South
Which is a bastion of racism.
President Obama continues to plod along despite
The daily criticism by the media and a drop-in ratings.

President Obama's Administration
Passed many important legislative acts
Since he became President.
The Health Care Reform Bill.
The Deployment of Troops to Iraq and Afghanistan.
Accepting General McChrystal's resignation.
The Appointment of General Petraeus
Commander of the Military Forces in Afghanistan.
The Financial Reform Bill which regulates the Banking System
In order to prevent another Financial Crisis.
The Extension of Unemployment Benefits to thousands of unemployed.

Despite these accomplishments
The Sea of faith which once enveloped him
Like a red shawl reaches its climax.
The journey is finished, the summit attained and barriers fell.
One thing is outstanding, the battle to be won
When the "Gordian Knot" of racism is untied.
Then we all will say, "Free at last, thank God we are free at last."

Thursday July 29, 2010

America

America, you are the most generous nation the world has ever known!
You fought with Allied forces in World War II from 1939–1945;
You have stemmed the pandemic of HIV;
You have supported the eradication of drugs in Colombia, Panama, Mexico,
Afghanistan, and many Central American countries.

America, you have singlehandedly destroyed the nucleus of terrorism, when
You killed Bin Laden, leader of Al Qaeda—The international terrorist organization.

Yet in many countries, the name America is like that of a Red Rag to a bull!
For thirty years you supported the Egyptian dictator, Hosni Mubarak.
For forty-two years you supported the Libyan dictator, Muammar el Gaddafi.
Both are military dictatorships.

We are told that America intervenes when America's interest is threatened.
This was not the case in Jamaica and Grenada.
In America, people are given permits to grow marijuana.
Yet America tries to eradicate it in some countries.
In America, smoking is banned in certain areas,
while manufacturers export their cigarettes to underdeveloped countries.

The type of Democracy that you are transporting to underdeveloped countries
is not right.
You push adult suffrage—one man, one vote—and freedom to vote in a polling
station without incident.
Yet when a leader is chosen in a fair election, you do not recognize the people's choice.
Government is an agent of the people; this can be changed whenever the
people wishes.
There is not one best form of government; government should vary with the
needs of the people.
America, we need a new type of Democracy. One size does not fit all.

Barack Obama Recipient of the 2009 Nobel Peace Prize.

Scientists can put men on the Moon and bring them back safely.
Can find a new planet and determine its course.
Barack Obama remains an enigma to his countrymen.
Inspires hope and confidence in many countries of the world.

Our faculties cannot comprehend what motivates this man.
Is it the desire to relieve the suffering of humanity?
Or a striving to perfect all human possibilities.

His critics feel he is describing a "Utopia."
He is convinced that his "Utopia" can make a difference.
It is attainable!
His reform will bring back the "golden age,"
When America was the dominant power in the world.

This is a "Bloodless Revolution."
The result is a downturn in the economy and massive unemployment.
Obama is saying to all his countrymen.
"America wants every citizen to do his duty!"
There will be a temporary rise in unemployment, but stay the course.

America, stand firm behind your leader.
Although unemployment and the economy will wear us out.
Never take a rest until victory is achieved.
The sweet fruition of a job well done.
That perfect bliss that only victory can bring.
Then all America will join hands with the Nobel Peace Prize Committee
And say this premature award is justified.
We knew he would have done it.

Monday, November 02, 2009

Birds

I do believe that birds have a message
In their chirps
I am convinced of this.

One Saturday morning, a bird wandered into my bedroom
I was surprised indeed.
No window or door was open.

I frantically opened the windows and doors
To facilitate his departure.
Instead he fluttered from wall to wall still chirping.

What melody! Enriched by each flutter of his wings.
I do not understand your message.
But fly my greetings, speeches, and smiles
To the other world from which you came.

Tuesday May 12, 2010

Cholera in Haiti

Haiti is besieged by tragedy!
The latest is cholera!
Three hundred and sixteen thousand dead.
Millions living in tent cities.
Everyone knew this would happen!
Because of poor sanitation after the January 12th earthquake
And flood from the rainy season.

Beside to date, only five percent of the ruins
The quake left behind has been cleared.
This in not only a hindrance to the rebuilding process,
But it is a safety hazard.

The Presidential elections with its long history
Of unjust government helped to fan the flames of discontent.
Young people with rocks in their hands
Marched in droves in the streets,
Pelting stones at the United Nation Mission.
Who are blamed for bringing the Cholera Virus to Haiti?

After the earthquake, Billions of dollars were pledged to Haiti's reconstruction.
Some countries made good their pledge.
Brazil, Norway, Estonia and Australia.
Altogether about $500 million has been disbursed.
Many countries are still behind with their pledges;
Many feel that the funds are misappropriated.
Lord, how long will Haitians suffer!
What reinforcement will they get from Hope?
What resolution from despair?
God, please send help quickly!

Monday, January 24, 2011

Boots

Boots.
Masculine, sturdy.
Walk, run, stamp.
Tattered, torn, dirty, and damp.
Boots.

Angels

Angels.
Heavenly, winged.
Flies, floats, and hovers.
Glorious, holy, joyful, peaceful.
Angels.

Monday, November 02, 2009

Come Quickly

Michael Manley! You should be living now,
Jamaica needs you.
To witness the country that you loved,
Thrashed by violence.
Gun-toting hungry-belly mob that ravished
Tivoli Gardens and most of Western Kingston.
March in the street with pride.

Rise up! Return to use soon;
Help us realize a country flowing with jobs,
Of children dressed for school with hope in their eyes
And proud parents going to work.
You were an inspiration to all.
We can still hear your voice
Saying you can do it.
Come, Mike! Come soon!

Sunday, June 27, 2010

DEATH

I have to think of death,
Whether I want to or not.
Every day I am reminded
If you die, I don't know:
If you have a bank account!
If you have a will!
My response is "You may die before me."
Alternating with "All men must die."
I will never tell them where I hid my treasures.
Because all criticized me when I was working hard.
"When I have fears that I might cease to be"
I get in a pensive mood and reflect.
"Death will come when thou art dead, soon, too soon."
Death thou art a welcome guest. Whenever you come.

Monday April 5, 2010

Dem ole im

Bwoy dem ketch im!
Wo! Dudus, yu no hear!
Bwoy yu lie! Mek a tell yu 'bout de news
For all im do fe we!
Jamaica mek im gone a America
Dat no any trial!
Dat a slayin of an inocent man.
Yu a tell mi all de 76 brethren
Wo dead in Tivoli Garden dead fe notin
Dat no fair.
Dat is a blessed man!

Gad no, im no do all dat dem say im do
Dat man give all we need in dis time of tribulation.
Yu si de man Goldin se im a prime minister
Wen wi done wid im, e we will be prime mutton.
Dudus is a good man
Let's all get togedda and kill all Americans
Let we tell Bruce Goldin some ting!
Black man a cry! We leada is dead!
Black man qwine eat crow now!
Two million American can't make up
For wat dem do to im.

Sunday,
June 27, 2010

Discontent

Sometimes I feel discontented
When I think I will never see my homeland again.
Although my way of life is much better here with the luxuries of life.
Meat or chicken every day.
Ham and eggs for breakfast.
All the fruit juices you can think of.
Orange, mango, grape, and nectarine.

Oh! How I long for a cup of chocolate tea with coconut milk.
Hard dough bread with salt margarine.
Crackers with guava jam at breakfast.
Salt mackerel and banana at dinner.
Oh! I am really discontented in the lap of luxury.

I shall return to see those people going to the market.
With their produce on their donkeys.
And baskets on their heads.
They are so well mannered.
"Morning, morning" to everyone they meet.
The beaches with the fishermen
And their baskets selling their catch.
The women calling, "Booby eggs, booby eggs."

Nothing can quell the desire to go home.
I don't know what each day holds.
All I know, one day I will go home.

09-29-2008

1. Should Muammar Gaddafi be denied the hospitality of the American people when he was a guest of the United Nations?

2. Should Roman Polanski be extradited after pleading guilty to unlawful sexual intercourse?

3. Should the President of the United States take time off his busy schedule to canvas the Olympic Committee for the 2016 Olympic Games?

Disgusted with Old Age

Oh, for a draft of rum
So that I might ruminate in a quiet place
A place where I can collect my thoughts
And know my self
A place where I can reflect on past failures.

A place where in the quiet
I can ask forgiveness for my sins, which are many
But more than all, a quiet place to contemplate
Old age because it has robbed me
Of the basic faculties that made me human.

I hate old age, I really do!
I can't remember recent events
And I fear when I deteriorate
I will not remember past events.

Oh God, walk with me each day
Steer me from critical people and hectic places
Then will I remember the nice things you said about old age.

Egypt

Egypt, for thirty years you have been mired down
By a dictator—Hosni Mubarak and his
Supreme Council of the Armed Forces.
What cause the populace to rebel now?
Is it because of the successful overthrow of?
The government in Tunisia by the people?
Or was it a flash! Now is the accepted time?
Let's go for it!

The people have the essentials for a protest.
But they have no leader—
Only spurred on by the social media.
The protesters decided to march in a peaceful
Manner—no violence!

These are the demands of the people:
Parliament must be dissolved.
Reform of the Constitution.
The power of the President must be curtailed.
Repeal of the laws that limit independent candidates.
Fair elections.
Allow wider political Freedom.
The inclusion of the opposition groups, i.e., The Muslim Brotherhood.

The protestors kept their promise of non-violence.
Things changed! When the military moved into Tahrin Square,
The epicenter of the uprising in Cairo,
Tents were destroyed; there were casualties and loss of life.
"Push on, push on!" was the battle cry!
They sprung to vengeance with an easy pace.
Blind to fate and cursed forever if the "Revolution" fails.
Victory at last!

There was mutual agreement on some of their demands.
The protestors agreed to continue their discussion.
Until all their demands are addressed.
Lovers of Democracy all over the world.
Applauded the effectiveness of nonviolence protest.
"The World's great age begins anew."
Democracy has come to the Middle East.
Rudimentary though it be.

Wednesday February 22, 2011

Election Results

Be not dismayed by the midterm election results of 2010.
Failure portends future success.
As long as total defeat is not assured
The future bodes well for victory.

Tuesday November 1, 2010

Fear

Do not fear what lies ahead.
He will hide you under the shadow
Of his wings.
He will guide you in the path of righteousness.
Because his mercies are for them
Who walks in his ways

Tuesday March 8, 2011

Final Assault

Once more the President mounts a final assault.
To get Health Care for all Americans.
The Republicans will not help.
The Democrats are divided.

The Republicans chant their song:
"Start all over again."
All efforts to get the bill passed are greeted with skepticism.
Pass procedural maneuvers are tabooed.

The President finds comfort in himself and his cause.
And while the mortal clouds are gathering,
He stands firm.
America, stand firm behind your President!

The bill with all its flaws will help millions of Americans get health care.
Americans, have you no hope!
To do nothing is to fail!
If we fail, all of us fail!
The President and the Nation
Will the President prevail? Yes!
This is he, whom every man in America should want to be.
Friday, March 19, 2010

Fisherman

Oh! What's the matter? What's the matter, fisherman?
He looked steadfastly at the tranquil sea.
Hopeless, helpless.
As he ponders his future
While brown-black scum
Slides helplessly, quietly along.

What does the future
Hold? For he and his family
No fish, no shrimp, no oysters,
No turtle, no crab.
Eleven men are all dead
What then?

BP must be made to pay.
For the damage that it has done.
How long will that suffice. ,
When a man's livelihood is taken from him.
The President has pledged his support
To get compensation for all.
'Tis little, very little—all
They can do for us.

Tuesday June 15, 2010

Forgetfulness

So much I have forgotten since I come to Georgia.
So much I have forgotten in ten years.
Forget what I had for breakfast.
Forget what time of day it is.
Forget to take my pills.
Forget the names of friends and neighbors.
Forget where I hide my bonds and cultured pearls.
Forget to check the back yard of the house I brought.
When I go home for vacation, I
Forget the name of the street and bus.
Sometimes I wonder what is happening to me.
I can remember things that happen when I was a child
But recent things I have no recollection of!

Instead of dwelling on what was
I count my blessing, one by one.
Daily as I go and hope that
God will help me face each problem as I go.
Youth is no longer here or there
Youth, I bid thee a fond adieu, adieu!

Friday January 29, 2010

Freedom Has Many Hats

Freedom has many hats.
Freedoms to love one's neighbor as one's self.
Freedom to worship.
Freedom to choose one's faith.
Freedom to press along when plans fail, and hope is almost lost.
Freedom to triumph in disappointment, troubles, and sorrows.
Freedom to live in a free society.
Freedom to vote.
Lord, take all my freedoms, my memory, my understanding and my will.
Then I will be free at last to enjoy my many freedoms.

10/07/2009

Freedom

Poverty does not a pauper make
Nor wealth a rich man.
What then does each have in common—Freedom?
Freedom to choose which course to take to accomplish his goals
But foist a commitment to each man
To love himself and his neighbor as himself
Both become a slave to faith
But in that slavery
Each has an opportunity to validate his choice.

From the Project to the Presidency

Here comes a young man from Hawaii!
Salinsky in his hand.
Walking the Chicago projects
His armor, "Hope."
To improve the lot of people
With no future.

Here comes a young man from Hawaii!
His heart filled with determination to succeed.
He started the right way.

Columbia University, here he comes!
Then grounded with that knowledge.
He wondered what his next step should be.
Harvard, here he comes!
The quest for armament was complete.

How can he reach his goal!
He became an organizer.
In the project of Chicago.
His responsibility was to assist people in the project.
To articulate their problems
In order to get help to improve their status
From Private enterprise and government.
A measure of success!

Ah, happy chance!
To challenge an incumbent for her seat
In Chicago House of Representative.
But failure raised its horny head.
Get hence; get hence! Failure!
Here comes another opportunity!

Oh, luck! You have come at last!
He won a seat in the legislature
By questionable maneuvers
That made all his future strategy complete.
"Only reapers reap early."
The Presidency, here I come.
The White House, the First Black President.
That is the final goal.

Tuesday November 2, 2010

Goodbye My Son

Goodbye, my son.
You have long passed your stay.
You always say that I abandoned you
When you were a child.
Now is my time!

At the age of twenty-three
You returned to live with me.
You went to college
And graduated with a Master's Degree.
Paid for by me!

With that success
You left without saying thanks
During those years you communicated sporadically.
I got an urgent call
Asking me to assist you.
This I did gladly.

You returned home.
You are now living with me.
Twenty-nine years.
During those years
You assisted with domestic chores at your pleasure
We had no confrontation.
But I still think
It is time for you to go
This is my time?
Revenge is sweet.
It is sweet
Whether you are the revenge
Or the revenger.

I will shed no tears when you are gone
Fruits are not ripe until their season.
Now is my time! Be gone!
Justice, thou are come at last!
Thank God you have come!

Thursday February 04, 2010

Haiti After the Earthquake

Tens of thousands of people killed!
Thousands displaced on January 12th.
When the worse earthquake in two hundred years hit Haiti.

The grim aftermath shocked the world!
Thousands of casualties untreated.
Disease results from untreated wounds and water.
Lack of bandages, splints, vaccines, antiseptics
Operating rooms not operable due to lack of Supplies and personnel.
Emergency vehicles can't get through the streets
Missionaries accused of kidnapping
And Trafficking in Children.

Where is all the money gone?
When the tragedy occurred
International donors pledged $5.3 billion.
Four countries make good their pledge.
Brazil, Norway, Estonia, and Australia
Altogether about $506 million has been disbursed.

America has not paid up yet!
Bill Clinton, United Nations, Special Envoy to Haiti
Is encouraging Nations to send in their pledges.
Haiti urgently needs your help.
Send you pledge as quickly as you can
Send it now!

Sunday August 29, 2010

Haiti

Haiti was destroyed by the worse earthquake in modern times.
The disaster is etched in the minds of all who saw its aftermath
Dead! Dead! Dead!

Nowhere to bury the dead.
Greave no more, a mass grave is ready.
Thousands and Thousands of bodies are ready to be put away.

With heavy thump, the lifeless bodies dropped one by one.
Shovel by shovel until the trucks were empty.
Leaving only the stench of death behind.

Everyone left the scene in a hurry
To pursue other acts of charity.
Only the dead stood together.
No one said a word of prayer.
There was no objection from the grave!
Only the lament from bystanders
That the corpses didn't have individual graves.

Rescue by dogs and their handlers continued with some success
Doctors treated the casualties
Orphans are put in homes or relocated.
What does the future hold for Haiti?

Despite her checkered history of slavery,
Dictatorship and weak Democratic governments,
Haitians will build again
Haiti shall never be vanquished!
God bless you in your endeavors.

Monday February 8, 2010

Haitians Celebrate

It's one month since the earth quaked.
Today, thousands marched and danced in the streets.
As they recalled the day
Port-au-Prince was raised to the ground.

Two hundred years ago the same thing happened!
It is difficult to compare devastations.
It is difficult to compare then and now.
Some may out live this catastrophic time.

When wasteful natural disaster
Make rubble of buildings and overturn statues
Leaving vast amounts of masonry and misery behind
The landscape looked savaged by Armageddon

Against death and all other destructive force
Haiti shall shine more brightly than before.

03/01/2010

Hope

Lord, for many years
I have waited for you
To answer my prayer.
My faith grows weaker.
As the years go by.
It's just that I feel so vulnerable

I have bared my soul to you.
It's not that I am negative.
But there was nothing to be positive about.
Lord, I am sorry if I have offended you.

Friends say my circumstance is God's will for me.
I can't accept that reason!
I have feasted on his words all of my life.
I can't believe that he abandoned me.

I must console myself.
Life is just a journey that everyone must take
Sometimes it's strewn with difficulties.
That can't be understood.
Despite this, I must continue to believe.
He will come through for me!

What is Hope? But the belief that God
Will keep his promise of Eternal Life
"Hope springs Eternal in the Human Breast."

It's Not My Cup of Tea

What are you doing next weekend?
Nothing exciting, why?
Let's go to a "Tea Party meeting"
In Washington

"The Tea Party" is a group of people
From all walks of life.
Republicans and Independents.
Who think they can change the political culture.

The group was about eight hundred.
Everyone was shouting:
"Liberty not tyranny. Kill the bill"
The excitement was threatening.

Alone! All alone!
We were two of a kind!
We were Democrats who went to snoop.
We moved in the crowd cautiously.

The banners tell the story:
"Defend the constitution and freedom."
"The movement is for taking back our country."
"GOP candidates courting Tea Party votes in Primary Race"
"SC Lt. Gov. wants constitutional convention to repeal Health Care Law"
The goal: Obama must be a one-term President.
"Fortune may reverse her tricky plays"

Monday April 5, 2010

Joy

Joy! Joy in my heart.

Joy when I behold nature in bloom.

Joy when I put on my best dress.

Joy when I behold the stars in all their glory.
Joy to share God's gift of love.

Joy when sorrow lingers.

Joy is peace beyond measure.

Joy is God's gift and so divine.

Monday, November 02, 2009

Longing for Peace

Many persons laud the efficacy of prayer.
But I can't say that's my experience.
I pray to start my day.
I pray forgiveness of my sins every day.

In all these instances, I have seen no change.
Will there be a new day for me?
The sun will rise tomorrow,
But I am certain it will be the same as before.

Is hope gone?
I think not.
I have faith!
My faith is the belief that God will intercede on my behalf someday.

Lord, help me strive to see that day.
When my body will be reviewed and my mind released from care.

03/01/2010

Massachusetts

Massachusetts, I am surprised
At your choice of a Senator.
You have turned the sweat years of Uncle Teddy
Into a disaster for the whole country.

All that he had worked for
Forty-seven years.
Was dashed out of the window
For some form of party strife.
Strife which has its objective
To ensure Barack Obama is a one-term President.

Is American electorate so fragile?
That they feel that all campaign promises
Must be realized in one year?
Are Americans so blind
That they can't read international economic trends?
What is the value of free trade, and small government?
When fifty thousand Americans are without jobs,
Without healthcare.
A long, bloody war in Afghanistan is not advantageous.

How can America Continue?
Disarmament efforts, narcotic control,
Famine relief, and subsidizing failing democracies.
Al Qaeda is emboldened and determined
To strike out at America.

Terrorism must be controlled.
This has to be a corporative effort
For Democrats and Republicans.

Instead of plotting to undermine the President
Mr. Brown would be better off learning the skills
That make an effective Senator.

Barack Obama may well be a one-term President.
History will be the judge!
All the domestic political forces
Are like ravenous wolves in a pack;
Ready to pounce upon him with no pity.

Strong kings have fallen.
Empires have self-destruct.
Have Patience!
All the enemies will fall!
There will be respite for everyone.
Barack Obama will be triumphant in his efforts of reform.
The opposition will be exhausted with anger.
They have not succeeded in destroying him.
Their failure is their "Waterloo."

Friday January 29, 2010

Michael Jackson

Gone, Gone, Gone
I would that I could say more
But sadness envelopes me like a shroud
I reached for one of his records, but I found none.
I looked at the television and
There he was with his brothers, singing
"Where there is love, I will be there."
I groaned in grief and agony.
Why did you do this to yourself?
Why did you leave your family, friends, and fans so hastily?

The loss is common to our race
The circumstances of his death are common, to our time.
The facts do not quell my sadness.
It made my sadness even more.

Everyone who knew him well, knew that
This would happen someday.
The genuine relatives and friends warned him
But there were a few friends who exploited
His good nature for pecuniary gains.
Now they are wringing their hands.
Is it because of the loss of a dear friend?
Or the loss of monetary gains?

What caused this August?
What caused promoters, songwriters,
Arrangers from all over the world with
One accord recognized his work and
Many declared that his legacy will be
Revered for years to come

For a man whose personal life was
Checkered with many incidents of
An appalling nature
We will never know what really caused
Him to go on this destructive quest.
Shed no more tears, take off your
Cloak of sadness.
We are confident; he "will be there."
In an atmosphere of love and truth.
He will sing and dance in
The New Jerusalem.
Death did him proud!
September 2009

Mid Term Elections 2010 – Part 1

Republicans!
Energized by the "Tea Party" movement.
Purpose to ensure that President Barack Obama.
Is a one-term President.
With that objective, they all unite.
The airwaves, cable television, and Print Press.
Book writers voice their criticism as well.
This is a dangerous situation!
This will potentially create a climate
That will be threatening to the President and his family.
America, the world is watching you!
It will be a sad day for America and the world if you
Kill the first black President.

Monday January 25, 2011

Mid Term Elections 2010 – Part 2

R Republicans!

E Energized by the "Tea Party" movement.

P Purpose to ensure that President Barack Obama is a one-term President.

U United in the cause they all unite.

B But if you pause to contemplate.

L Let us go to God in prayer.

I I know that he will answer all our prayers.

C Calm our fears; this will pass away.

A Anxiety can bring us down and destroy us!

N May God help us all, to find common ground.

Wednesday, November 24, 2010

Oil Spill

Oil! Oil! Everywhere!
On the sea, coastline, marshlands, and beaches.
The BP oil rig blew up; eleven men lost their lives.
Dead were fishes, shrimps, oysters, crabs, turtles, birds
And countless animals trapped in the deep.

From selected areas on the sea, black smoke.
Bright red, yellow flames deliberately ignited,
To burn the oil, can be seen for miles.

Thousands of workers employed to.
Clean up the oil.
Carry sticks, rakes, and bags and,
Decontaminated birds drenched with oil.
This was the worst oil disaster in America.

BP CEO, Tony Hayward, cool, calm, and collected.
Sat alone around a table waiting to answer questions
While members of the Energy Sub Committee,
Like a hungry pack of wolves, poised to ask questions.

None of the questions got a productive response.
This angered the committee.
Many resorted to conjecture.
The consensus was that the nonproductive response
Was due to impending litigations with the government.

The hearing had its memorable moments.
A brawl by demonstrators.
But the most astounding moment!
Republican Joe Barton apologized to BP.
He called the Twenty Billion dollars fund

Set up by President Obama with BP to pay reparations "a shakedown"
Engineered by the government and Paid for by BP.

Joe Barton Republican of Texas retracted his apology
After being threatened by his colleagues to lose his senior position on the committee.
Nothing was accomplished by the committee.
Was this a triumph of Big Oil?
Only time will tell!

Saturday, June 19, 2010

Playful Pals

Sleeping dog and watchful cat.
Dog sleeping and pal cat appears ready to pounce.
Unless prey comes, both will maintain their stance.
Dear God, Send them prey.

Monday, November 02, 2009

Quatrain 1

Life is a game.
Uncertain is the dice.
Remember an unfair game.
Always plays twice.

Age is full of pain and woe.
It's like winter all year round.
Cold and limp in its response.
It seems to stay all too long.

Tuesday October 5, 2010

Quatrain 2

How should one respond to death's approaching stride?
Fear the future and what it holds.
Sing a song of fond farewell.
Or pray for the repose of the soul.

I heard a friend is dying.
Lord, help him to repent.
He has destroyed so many lives.
I wish him Godspeed.

Tuesday October 5, 2010

Quietness

It is so quiet.
I can hear myself breathing.
The quietness is foreboding.
The trees stand tall, like soldiers at their posts.
The leaves are not dancing in the breeze.
No bird sings.
The scene enhances the quiet darkness of the sky.
Is there a pending storm?
The forecast does not say.
What could it be?
As I try to understand the landscape.
Past memories are unremembered.
Pleasure floods my mind.
Am I the cause of this quietness?
Maybe, who knows?
All I know that time has passed.
The best portion of life has passed.
Despite this, let's remember acts of kindness and of love.
These will lift the quietness of the soul.

Realization

Shirley Sherrod! Have you heard of her?
I can't say I have!
Shirley Sherrod was a rural development officer,
Employed by the Department of Agriculture,
Who was asked to resign after videotape comments
She made in March at a local NAACP banquet
Surfaced on the web
Quickly spread to cable and broadcast news.

This story, Sherrod told many times.
The interaction was with a white farmer in 1986
Who faced foreclosure on his farm.
This incident changed her attitude towards
The "black and white" situation.
She realized that it was not "black against white"
But was "rich versus poor."
As a result she changed her attitude towards
The "Black" and "White" issue.

She reiterated the story because the NAACP
Convention attacked the Tea Party movement.
It called on the movement to repudiate
Racist elements within its ranks.
Sherrod feels that all people, would have to
Live and work together
This goal cannot be accomplished in a minute
That is why she shared her steps to transformation.

The Under Secretary of Agriculture, Cheryl Cook
Informed her that the "White House" required her
Resignation. Sherrod tendered her resignation;
Tom Vilsack, Secretary of Agriculture, accepted

Her resignation.
He apologized for the inconvenience to which she was subjected
He offered her a post in Washington, DC.

However, controversy of another sort erupted.
Would President Obama offer her an apology?
He did! She accepted!

When President Obama intervened in the
Racially motivated incident with
His friend Professor Louis Gates, of Harvard,
President Obama requested that all of the
Parties involved come to the "White House"
For a beer.
It would appear Sherrod will not be
Invited to the "White House."

Where is the audacity of hope?
Where is the new paradigm of power?
Love and justice!
Are we all disillusioned?

It would appear that people black and
White must continue the Struggle
For racial equality; let's not harbor a divided
Thought, but go to the deliberation with the determination to succeed.
It is not too late to catch a fallen star.

Wednesday, July 28, 2010

Reflection - 1

I don't want to die here. I don't.
I don't want to die among strange people
With their subtle hatred for foreigners.
Let me go back to the poverty and violence
Because that's where I belong.
That's where my soul will find peace and rest
Because that's where I belong.

It was nice at first when I was young
Vibrant and preoccupied with success.
New York was the place to be.
I always say if you can't make it in that city
You can't make it anywhere.
But what a price?

Now I am sick and handicapped
My motto is still the same, "I must make it."
In my present state, what is success?
Just getting out of bed! Can you believe that!
Yes! Where the tree falls, there will it lie.

It is as I have said, "I don't want to die here."
Let me go where my ancestral spirits will greet me.
Through joy or grief, through pain or pleasure
They will be there to say, "Well done, my child,
You are a success."
My heart's in my homeland far, far away
There, my loved ones are waiting to welcome me home.
Through joy or grief, through pain or pleasure
They will be there to say, "Well done, my child,
You are a success."

August 25, 2009

Reflection - 2

When I think of how I spent my life
Tears trickle down my cheeks.
Lord, let me remember all my sins
So that I can repent in peace.

What a life!
What a record.
What multi-colored memories?
Nothing can erase those memories.

As I pace forth in my room
I feel there is redemption for me.
Sometimes I look upon myself and curse faith.
Why? When I followed my heart.

Let me learn from my mistakes.
Lord, prepare me for the days ahead.

03/01/2010

Republicans!

Republicans
Energized by the "Tea Party"
Purpose to ensure that President Barak Obama is a one-term President
United are we in the pursuit of destruction
Before the election in 2012, we will destroy President Barak Obama's chance
for election.
Let all our representative in Washington, DC, continue to obstruct legislation
It's difficult to explain why there are so many candidates in the Presidential race.
Candidates must be Zealots to the cause of President Barak Obama's destruction.
All members of the party must stand as a cohesive group if President Barak
Obama is to
      Be destroyed.
Now unto the breach dear members!

November 24, 2010

Shout

S – Shout for joy!

H – Hope in God's love when life hurts.

O – Oh, give me joy forever.

U – You are the salt of the earth.

T – Tell it to Jesus alone.

Monday, November 02, 2009

Sleep

Sleep, you have eluded me for many years.
You have been an unwelcomed guest of my father and brother.
Now me, Why?

Oh! How I wish that I could sleep at night.
What have I done to deserve this fate?
What can I do to defend against this vicious enemy?

Twelve, One, Two, Three and sometimes Four a.m.
No sleep! And in those hours my thoughts run wild.
Here comes the morning!
With its groggy and depressed feeling.

Must I pretend that I slept well last night?
God forbid!
Sleep, you are such a gentle thing.
Oh! How I wish that you would slide into my soul.
Then I will arise and hug the dawn
What a day!

Tuesday, June 08, 2010

Spring

Spring is here, pause and look.
I know it because the trees tell.
Tall, Majestic green trees;
Decked with twinning green leaves
Space out in the fields
As if they were planted

Trees reaching up to the sky
On hillside and valleys.
Trees reflecting God's glory etched and still.
As I pass this way each morning,
And view this beautiful scene.
I sense the presence of God in all creation.
Thank God, His gift abides with us.

Tuesday, May 25, 2010

Synopsis

The devastation seen in Haiti because of the earthquake is heartrending.
People without food, water, and medical attention.
Children separated from their parents.
No graves to bury the dead.

This poem is like a record of the tragedy. The description is very graphic so
That the reader can envisage the tragedy.
 The march in the street to celebrate the anniversary of one month,
 Shows how resilient the Haitian people are.

Friday, March 19, 2010

Terrorism

September 11, 2001.
Brings to the consciousness the destructive force of terrorism.
American Airlines Flight 11 crashed into the First Tower of the World Trade Center
In New York City.
United Airlines Flight 175 crashed into the Second Tower of the World Trade Center
In New York City.
American Airlines Flight 77 crashed into the Pentagon
In Washington, DC
United Airlines Flight 93 crashed into the empty lot
In Pennsylvania.

President George W. Bush shaken by the attacks.
Stated that the United States was engaged
In a global war on Terror.
Radical Islam is ready to exterminate the infidels.
In Response, America occupied Afghanistan.
That was a just action!

Afghanistan had sheltered Al Qaeda
Iraq was not involved.
Yet Iraq was invaded.
Was there a mischaracterization of events?
By President George Bush.
Or was it war fever at its highest!
Now many are questioning the global war on Terrorism.

Is the present strategy correct?
I think Al Qaeda is like a franchise.
It determines the political and ideological
Objectives of the organization.

But each cell can determine the way it meets
The goals of the organization.

Taking into account the country's terrain
Its own tribal hierarchy
Its experience with democracy
The economics of the country.

Can we call everyone who is engaged
In death and destruction a terrorist?
Are there no freedom fighters anymore?
When the Palestinians selected a president
By popular and fair voting
Israel refused to negotiate with him.
Instead they choose to negotiate with
Mahmoud Abbas, who was not the people's choice

If peace is to be a reality
We must respect the people's choice.
All I know, this massive destruction
All over the world will not achieve peace.
What shall we do?
Wait for the fulfillment of prophesy of Jeremiah 32: 37-38.

"I will bring them back to this place, and I will
Cause them to dwell safely. They shall be my
People and I will be their God."
God said to Abraham, "And also of the son
Of the bondwoman will I make a nation,
Because he is thy seed."
To Hagar Mother Ishmael, the angel of God
Said, "I will make him a great nation."

The End of an Era

One of the finest warriors on the
American political battlefield is dead.
Words of condolence was sent from all
Parts of the world and all over the United
States of America, which he served for forty-
Seven years.

The poor wept because their champion was dead
The poor wept because their hope for Health Care
Reform is almost dead.
The poor wept because the hope of progressive
Legislation to improve the quality of life for all
Americans is dead.

The rich never asked how they can build a
Better America
Instead they seek to speculate who in the
Kennedy dynasty will succeed Uncle Teddy.
We do not know who it will be, but all we
Know someone will come from that
Family to serve America.

Wait, sing no dirge!
Teddy Kennedy said, "The hope lives on"
We must build a better America.
Uncle Teddy hand-picked Barack Obama
To carry the torch to victory
Let us all hold the banner high and
March to a new drummer of hope and
Change

Uncle Teddy, we say goodbye.
Thanks for all the good things you did
For us
'Tis hard to part with a friend so dear.
But we are confident, we will see
You again in some brighter clime.

August 25, 2009

The Hour Has Come

"Health Care Reform" was attempted
By many American Presidents without success.
Now it's President Barack Obama's turn
To put his hands on the wheel.

Opposition came from every direction.
From his own party, The Democrats.
The Republicans defy any efforts
To work in a bipartisan way.

Hope was almost gone!
After one year of rebuff by the Political parties and segments of the nation
It was time to take off
Time to revamp and to recoup.

There is no leadership!
"Where is our leader?" the Democrats cried!
"It seems as if we have all been denied.
Come, let us find him where here he abides, because he has told us a dreadful lie."

But wait! Wait!
Here comes the President with a blue print.
A final assault on the Health Care Reform Bill.
The vehemence of the nation has not abated
The "Tea Party" members joined by countless, voiceless, hopeless comrades.
Marched outside "The Commons"
Intimidating Congress Persons with racial and homosexual slurs.

The President came to encourage the Democrats for the Final Vote
The President said, "The Health Care Reform Bill
Is the great unfinished business in our society;
Vote for what is right and true."

The Health Care Reform Bill was passed
By 221 members of Congress
The President signed it into law on 3/23/2010.
Thus ending a century of failures.

Tuesday March 23, 2010

The President Is in Danger

History will be the final arbiter of
President Obama and his administration.
His actions are governed by a fix mark:
His vision to bring hope and prosperity to his countrymen.

To bring hope to a country engaged in two wars.
To bring together conflicting political interests.
To foster bipartisanship between Democrats and Republicans.
To reduce the deficit.
To assure health care to all Americans.
To regain America's dominance in the world.
To restore America's financial integrity in the world.
To ensure economic stability at home.
To eradicate terrorism at home and abroad.

What hinders the President from achieving his goals?
Disdaining fortune with his stubbornness to intervene
In a National discussion on racism and where he was born!
His promise was like a morning star.
It shines so brightly.
Now after eighteen months in office
His opposition has turned the whole country against him.

Radio and Television pundits
Forecast that he will be a one-term President.
What cause love to turn to despair?
Opposition supporters wear "T-Shirts" stating
"Let his days be few, and let another
Take his office.
Let his children be fatherless and
His wife a widow."

Now promise is so dim and fear rises high.
The President and his family are in danger!
What can his supporters do?
The faithful will continue to support him.
President Obama has never wavered in
Loyalty to his vision and to America.
Let not history say to the
Faithless in your impatience you have
Forfeited a "new day."

Sunday August 29, 2010

The Time Has Come – I

Blow, Trumpet! Blow!
America wants to discuss racism!
There is a deafening clamor all across America.
The battle cry is "The time is opportune"
Blow, Trumpet! Blow!

There is a problem!
Many African Americans think the President should convene the talks.
It is their observation that the President does not like to discuss "race."
As a result, teachable moments are lost
Blow, Trumpet! Blow!

"Let sleeping dogs lie," Mr. President
God forbid!
The President is fettered with legal knowledge.
A former Professor of Constitutional Law.
An intellectual, A Noble Peace Laureate.
With all this armor, he is unable to remove from his people.
The grief that saps the mind radiates false pride, civic slander, and spite.
To engender in a people that have been oppressed, discredited all their lives,
Love of truth and righteousness.
Blow, Trumpet! Blow!

"Was the hope drunk" when we elected him, No!
African American intellectuals, civic leaders, and the church
Should come together and air their views on "Racism."
"Racism" is like a cancer in our society.
Blow, Trumpet! Blow!

If we should fail? We fail!
Let us not ascribe failure to our President.
Let's not become the servant of defeat.

Let's embrace the first African American President with peace and love.
He is a victim too.
Let him enjoy his success, because in it, we all
Rise with more hope than we had before.
Blow, Trumpet! Blow!
It is our hope that one day the Trumpet will be still.

Saturday, January 23, 2010

Tragedy at Fort Hood

No taps were heard.
Instead the rat-a-tat of gun shots and
The sirens of emergency vehicles blast
The quiet military compound.

Dead were twelve young soldiers preparing
To be deployed to Afghanistan.
One civilian, bringing the dead to thirteen
Causalities to thirty-five.

The officer who wrought this terrible deed,
Major. Dr. Nidal Malik Hasan, a psychiatrist
What caused this officer to turn on his comrades in this manner?
Is he a covert terrorist or a sick man?
Only time will tell.

In the meantime, radical Muslims
Celebrate his action.
They say Islam is against hatred.
Nationalism and Secularism is the
War cry in New York City.
The radicals envisaged a holy land
Stretching from Israel to Rome.

Dr. Hasan is recuperating from his rampage
In Brook Army Medical Center.
He is visited by Doctors and lawyers
Who are trying to find answers to this tragedy?

It will take months or years to unravel
The motivation behind this vicious attack.
However, the President assures us of
Swift Justice.

America, before you meet out swift and thorough justice,
Remember justice is a two-edged sword.
Major Hasan was born and bred in America.
He is a product of America and its culture.

Where did the military go wrong?
Is the Major's response due to
Sickness untreated for so long or
Is his response entirely due to military culture?
We hope the investigation will find the answer
Will paralysis to the upper and lower extremities
Be enough payment for this dastardly deed?

In the meantime, we must bid our soldiers rest.
There is no need for them to dream
Of the battlefield anymore.
No fear of days of danger and nights
Of being ambushed by the enemy.

You have earned your eternal rest.
Those whom you have left behind
Will secure justice for all of you
Because you have paid the ultimate sacrifice
In trying to ensure freedom and peace
In a world of hate.

November 16, 2009

Tsunami

There is something truly majestic when
God's awful power is unleashed.
In the Twinkling of an eye, the 8.9 quake
Struck Japan, and shortly after, the Tsunami.
Stealthily moved with quiet ferocity,
Engulfing everything, everything in its path.
Homes, Cars, Vans, and People.

It was the most frightening scene to behold.
Man powerless to hold back the thick
Grey water moving quietly along.
It damaged the Nuclear Plants in
Fukushima Daiichi and Onagawa.

As a result, high levels of Radiation were found.
In the Milk, Green Vegetables, and in People
Living near the plant.
This caused fear in America that radiation
May reach coastal areas.

Japanese are doing everything in their power
To contain the damage
They have conferred with other friendly
Nations on various measures of containment.
They have sent out many Advisory to inform
The Nation and the World.

The Japanese people have much
To thank God for.
For the strength and courage of its people.
For even in the darkest times the people
Maintain their discipline in the midst of darkness

Loneliness and sorrow.
Things happen for a reason!
Let's hope that Nuclear-Powered Countries
May upgrade their Nuclear Plants to
Prevent the spill of Radiation.
And ensure a safer World.

Tuesday, March 29, 2011

Unjust World

That's my son Michael lying in bed with not a care in the world.
This upsets me tremendously.
When I consider how life has treated me
My soul cries out; there is no justice on this earth.
Am I to wait for death to obtain justice from the "Great I Am?"

I have been working from I was eighteen years old.
I had no respite until I was sixty-six years old.
Yet this boy has retired at forty-two years old and can't get a job.
What brought this about?
His betrayal by so-called friends.
That's what he said. But was It?
We will never know because there was no proceeding.

How then must we determine justice?
Must we take it in our own hands?
Or let the courts who should be just
Continue to rule unjustly on our behalf?
A man who satisfies the court's demands
Should at least be given a chance to work and contribute to society.

The system is weighted in its own brand of justice
So lives continue to be destroyed.
What hope is there for those that are unjustly charged?
They have paid in fines and probation.
What must a person who is mistreated by a corrupt system do?
Trust that somehow good will be the final goal of evil.
Or bottle up his anger in his breast until it
Over flows into an unsuspecting crowd.
Where's the justice when the wronged and the unsuspecting crowd
Pay the price of institutional injustice and unequal laws.

Little systems have their day and ultimately cease to be.
Our only response to this injustice is to increase our faith in God.
Faith and faith alone can embrace believing what we hope for
That good will fall to all.
Christ shall return to correct injustice.
"Tis not too late to seek a newer world."

Tuesday, December 01, 2009

Osama Bin Laden Is Dead

What caused jubilation in the street of USA,
England, Europe, and some Arab countries?
Usama Bin Laden is dead!
American, "You have scorched the snake, not killed it."

Al Qaeda, the organization which he founded,
Promised revenge!
Who will be their leader now?
Will the leader come from Yemen?
Or the USA, to ensure fluency in English and Arabic?
It does not really matter,
They are a band of terrorist resolved to destroy
America and its allies.

Bin Laden is in the grave.
After a life of terrorism, he sleeps well!
Nothing can touch him further.
What can USA and the World do now?
They must continue the difficult task
Of stamping out terrorism, root and branch.
There is comfort yet! They are assailable.

Death is a victory to those who have painstakingly
Plotted his capture for ten years.
But are they ready for the fallout!
The revolution in the Arab world is frightening.

Victory has temporally enhanced President Obamas
Stature, because his critics who derided his leadership
See him in a different light.
Will this incident affect President Obama re-election bid?
For a second term in office? NO!

But he as the awesome task to quell the quell the clamor
For validation of Bin Laden death.
At present he stands firm in his decision
Not to publish the photograph of Bin Laden's capture
This is the word to the wise "for those who thou think'st
Thou dust overthrow
Die not, poor death; nor yet canst thou kill me."

Tuesday, May 10, 2011

Walk Good.

Walk good, man!
Yu hear wha me say walk good!
Yu hurry like yu hear bout a job
No such luck!

Ten years now since mi nah wok
I always think yu was a wok
Cause yu always in a hurry
Stop it, man! Yu walk too fast
Fe a man witout a job
At you age yu nah get no job anywhey

Evrybody say mi mus think positive
Yu nuh see when mi walk
Mi have a stiff uppa lip
Mi nah watch yu lip whetha it sof or stif
But all I kno yu walk fast
Like yu goin to a job

Cheer up, mi brotha
Black man ah eat crow now a days
Take mi advice walk slow because yu will walk long
Walk good! Mi man, Walk good!

Weather Forecast

On Monday there was an ominous
Weather advisory forecasting a tornado.
When I looked outside, the sky was black!
The clouds were moving in a hurry!
I feared the worst: as the lighting flashed.
The thunder rolled.
 I waited with fear and trembling!
The tornado did not come.
Fear no more!
Nature was playing one of her tricky games!
That made me so happy and relieved.

Tuesday, March 8, 2011

Woman with Child After the Quake

It was a tragic sight to see.
People running in the streets.
Hopeless! Helpless! Powerless!

Help! Help! Can you hear me?
Come quickly, hurry, hurry!
The voice sounded sad and soft.

Large tears she shed.
She held her child on her breast.
Both eyes red with crying.

Another day's journey without food.
She walked wobbly, shoeless.
Babe in arm hoping food will come.

At last, a Samaritan arrives
With some food for her and her child.
Lord, bless the hand that gives us food.

Lord, we have a lot to thank you for.
So many thoughts went through her head.
This is the day that the Lord has made
We must rejoice and be glad.

Tuesday, May 12, 2010

February 02, 2010

Title of Speech:

Honduras political crisis.

Opening Statement:

Too much political ambition leads to a coup

Body:

Manual Zelaya was President of Honduras

From 27 January 2006–28 June 2009.

On June 2009, he was removed from office by the Army taken to the Air Force Base Hernan Acosta Mejia and sent into exile in Costa Rica

Reason for Coup

On September 15, 2008 – Zelaya failed to file a budget in Congress as required by the Constitution

Attempted to modify 1982 Honduran constitution by convening the Constituent assembly to draft a new constitution which would increase his time in office.

This illegal move was strongly opposed by the Honduran Congress, the Honduran Supreme Court, the Opposition parties and his own party (Partido Liberal) as they all alleged that his real motive was to increase his time in office.

Violated Supreme Court ruling that upheld a lower court ruling stating that Zelaya

Executive decree PCM-05-2009 for the National Institute to hold a national referendum

Asking voters whether they wanted the ballot (to convene a National Constituent Assembly for the purpose of writing a new constitution) is included in the November 2009 election was blocked.

Conclusion:

President Obama said:

"We believe that the coup was not legal and that President Zalaya remains President of Honduras."

Hilary Clinton, Raul Castro, and Hugo Chavez demanded that he be reinstated as President of Honduras.

Their demands were not achieved.

A Brighter Day

There's a brighter day that's coming:
November 6, 2012, when we go to vote for
The President and Vice President for a second
Four years in office.
However, when we look at where we are
Coming from Slavery, and where we are now,
A black President and his white running mate.
We must take time to think of past victories,
Recount the battles we have won, and
What the future holds.
President Barack Obama and Vice President
Joe Biden said that the road is not easy
But we are still hopeful and confident that they will
Correct the Economic decline, put everyone
Back to work who wants a job, and bring prosperity back to America.

Friday, September 07, 2012

A Man Is a Man

Man is made in the image and likeness of God.
When Adam and Eve sinned and lost Paradise,
The consequence was all men must die!
Out of love for man, God sent his son Jesus Christ
To justify man, and restore and regain Paradise.

In his doctrine of love, Jesus decreed that man
Must love his neighbor as himself.
Therefore, anyone experiencing honest poverty, which
Is not his fault, but due to a down turn in the economy
Should not be ashamed to expect assistance,
From Government or his neighbors.

That's why people elect representatives to go to
Congress, to enact laws and legislations to govern
The people, and provide services during a depression,
Or other disasters.

Where did we go wrong? The people who are
Selected to represent the electorate in Congress and the
Senate gets corrupted very easily. They get
A good salary and medical care and do very little
For it. Some of them get an inflated ego and treat
Their constituents with contempt.
In a short while they become rich and famous!
A man is a man, whether rich or poor.
His needs are the same.
He has to take care of his family and, as a
Result, needs the wherewithal to do so.

Government has a responsibility to support
A man and his family in times of hardship.

It doesn't matter what the assistance is called, i.e.,
Socialism. The Constitution is right; all men
Are created equal and have a right to liberty
And the pursuit of happiness.
A man is a man whether he is
Black or white. Each has the same needs.
And government has a responsibility to each.

May 16, 2012

Adam Smith, where are you?

The United States of America has changed!
Years ago, thousands of people from all over
The World, came to these shores, because everyone
Knew that America was a land of opportunity and hope.

Everyone knew if he worked hard,
He would get a piece of the pie.
In those days, it was as if the streets were paved with gold.
And everyone has the Midas touch.

Now the streets are filled with people seeking jobs.
Or standing in line for food or other handouts.
Signs on many churches state the time for lunch
And everyone is welcomed.

What caused this change?
Has capitalism failed?
Where are the free-market believers?
It is wrong to believe that all economic problems
Are caused by supply and demand.

Economics deals with human behavior.
In the disposal of scarce goods.
Economics is not responsible for the ethical choices people make.
The culprits are the investors;
Who control the energy future's market?
They determine the cost of gas!
It has nothing to do with President Obama.
All the President can do is to make Renewable Energy Systems Possible.

Monday March 5, 2012

Advice to Kate on Her Wedding Day

Kate, with outstretched arms we welcome you into the British Royal Family.
Kate, fortune made you cupid's bow.
And for a lasting effect, beside the force to capture William's heart.
Still keep the bow erect, the same acts that gained him.
Must have the power to maintain him.

Bill Clinton

It is a shame that President Bill Clinton had to defend
The first Black President of the USA, Barack Obama,
From the racist elements in this country.
There is a rumor that President Bill Clinton had a spat
With President Obama; however, his presentation at the
Convention was void of rancor, and appeared motivated
By a sincere desire to explain to the electorate, the
Magnitude of the broken economy that President Obama inherited,
And to assure the country that the President did all
The right things necessary to correct the Economic
Situation in the present and in the future.

The country wants validation. President Obama
Can't be pushed around by the Republican Party
And its affiliate, The Tea Party. He is a different
"Black Boy"; he is the President of the United States of America.
Whatever he has done to correct the economic downturn
Is well documented.

No one expected the people of the USA
Would elect a black man as President.
Now that the novelty has worn off, the Republicans
And their affiliates, The Tea Party, are resolved to
Push him out of the White House.
They thought that a back family occupying the
White House is a problem, and they have voted to
Destroy his presidency. President Bill Clinton is
A Democrat and a consummate politician.
He knows when his party needs a vote
He doesn't vote conscience;
When his party needs assistance to regain power, he must help!

Every Democrat is happy that President Bill Clinton
And President Jimmy Carter will do everything
In their power to see President Obama be re-elected for a second Term

Every Democrat must pray that President Bill Clinton
Will keep healthy to execute this humanitarian task.
America will love him; prosperity will remember him
And his effort to destroy the Bastille of racism and injustice

Tuesday, September 11, 2012

First Lady

Who is Michelle Obama?
What is she? That all America loves her.
She is blessed with grace, dignity, poise, and
Education that makes her a monument of delight.

What offices she holds?
Wife of President Barack OBAMA.
First African America Lady of the United States of America.
Mother of Malia and Sasha.
Daughter of the late Fraser and Mrs. Marion Robinson.
Sister of Craig Robinson.

We saw her upon nearer view,
A liberated woman, free to eloquently defend her
Husband's ability to lead for another four years and
Crystallize his vision for the United States of America.

Though the circumstances look rough with
Uncertainties, Your love will last whatever the outcome.
Think noble thoughts; all will be well when the
Economy booms again, and the United States of
America takes its place again in the International
Community of Nations. You will find the President
Worthier to be loved because both of you have achieved your goals.

Monday, September 10, 2012

Forty-Seven Percent

Mitt Romney, the Republican Presidential Nominee,
Is a wealthy man by all accounts.
He only fraternizes with Millionaires and Billionaires.
He inferred, "One never seems to gain his ends
By helping the sick, poor and welfare recipients.
These jobless, ambitionless scums! To help
Them would be to increase the deficit.
Who wants that? On the other hand, I am successful.
They can pull themselves out of poverty by their own bootstraps.
Forty-seven percent of the electorate have welfare
Mentality. President Obama is the cause of that!
He will go down in history as the welfare President.
I have to win! I promise to find a way giving the illusion that
I am helping the electorate! For me, the sign of
Repentance is a gift of Welfare to the poor and indigent.
After all, I am a Mormon Bishop!"

Sunday, September 23, 2012

God's Plan

Keep us on course through this trying period,
Re-election! Let us not be distracted by
Distortion of facts and disrespect to opponents.
Lead us to victory in November 06, 2012.
We need to go forward: to build again the economy,
Put people back to work, repair international relationships,
And to increase our Faith and Hope in President
Barack Obama and his administration.
That they will be given another four years to complete
The work they have begun. Nothing in life happens
By chance; it's all part of a plan!
President Barack Obama will return for another
Term, because it's God's plan!

Friday, September 07, 2012

He Is an American

He is an American!
He has said it and has shown
His birth certificate to prove
That he is an American!
That is greatly to his credit
For he might be a Kenyan!
Or Hawaiian or Indonesian!
But despite all temptations
To belong to other Nations
He remains an American!

Saturday, September 01, 2012

How to Find Pleasure in Old Age

God's creation is visible everywhere.
In land and sea.
In land is seen tall and stately trees, standing
Like sentinels with green vines hanging from them.
Enhancing their dignity. While the giant redwood
Tree radiates its glory.

In summer, when flowers bloom displaying
A variety of colors, white, pink, yellow, red,
And lavender. What a beauty to behold these
Many colored flowers dancing in the breeze
And blossoms' petals fall to scatter on the ground.

The sea with its multitude of animals and vegetation;
With its light blue, deep blue, and greenish water.
Covering a vast area as far as the eyes can see.
The sea always in motion, never relaxed, and the
Rolling switching sound only the sea can make.
Invokes in me a sense of peace and tranquility.

These are only two of God's creation.
There are many more to explore. If you look hard
For beauty, you will find it! You have time to do so.
Let your mantra be: This is the day that the Lord
Has made, be glad and rejoice in it. Life will be
A pleasure in your old age.

Sunday, April 30, 2012

In God's Hands

President Obama, you and your family
Are in God's Hands.
Have no fear.
If chance made you President,
Chance will give you another term.
You are in the prayer of those who love you.
God is for us all
He will dispense justice.
Campaign with courage and hope
And everything will be all right.

May 17, 2012

Less We Forget

We must not forget his steadfast faith,
And true intent, when he came to office in 2009.
His hope for change energized,
Black and White Americans.

We must not forget when he first began,
The weary life he knew and hours of travail:
To perfect, the Affordable Care Act, and
The agony of waiting for the
Supreme Court to render judgment.

We must not forget when he took office:
He inherited the worst recession in thirty years
The struggle with the Banking System,
The Auto Industry, Immigration Reform,
The loss in Housing Value and Stocks, and
International Terrorism

We must not forget his accomplishments.
The Affordable Care Act was declared constitutional
By the Supreme Court on 6/28/2012
President Obama called it a victory for the people.
"All over the country whose lives will be secure
Because of this law."

We must not forget:
Things that are already in effect:
Elimination of co-payment for preventive care.
Young adults up to twenty-six years are covered under their parents Insurance.
Children with health problems cannot be denied Insurance coverage.
Employers will pay fines if they don't cover workers.

Insurance Market will make it easy for small business
And individuals to get coverage.

We must not forget that three
Years ago he was our hope for change
We all then approved
His steadfast faith never wavered
We must not forget this!

Tuesday, July 22, 2012

Look to the Future

When you leave your footprint on your country,
And people feel that your contribution was of little
Worth, remember that the seed you planted
Has improved the lives of many people in your
Country and gives hope to millions more in the World.
Life has a way of pushing on to greater heights
And a brighter dawn and a brand-new path awaits you.

Wednesday August 08, 2012

Looking to the future with anger.

He is found on the political scene,
To be a flip flopper and all the report
On his conduct agree. In polite company, he would be
Called a purveyor of untruth, with regards to his
Wealth and his accomplishment in creating jobs in the
Private sector. As a CEO at Bain Capital from 1990–2001,
He appeared exceptionally successful. Not only did he
Acquired Personal wealth, for himself and his shareholders,
But he destroyed the workers who created that wealth.
They were laid off, denied severance pay, pension and
Their jobs outsourced to countries where labor is cheap.
But everything that he did, he did not leave any tangible
Record to show how he destroyed the American Workers
And the economy. The press has mixed feelings. Some
See him as an opportunist intent on establishing
An Oligarchy of the Rich, and denying the Poor the opportunity
To move up in the Middle Class. The other segment of
The press is sympathetic to the plight of the Poor.

If Mitt Romney wins, it will be a victory for the rich.
The poor will be vanquished; Trade Unions will be destroyed.
There will be cuts in Social Services, which will affect
Food stamps, TANF, and Medicare will become
A voucher program. The future seems bleak for the poor.
If educational programs are cut, the poor will be unable
To meet the employment standards. The prisons will be
Full. Thousands will lose their right to vote and thus
Unable to change the system. The outcry will be Democracy
 Has failed.

Thursday, August 23, 2012

Mitt Romney and His Income Tax Returns

Stormy clouds are forming day by day.
Mitt Romney's problems seem to grow each and every day.
No answers on the way.
No hope for resolution.
No prayer is being said.

What will party colleagues do?
Split into Tea Party stalwarts,
Right Wing conservatives, Left Wing
Conservatives, or Centrists. Or will a new
Category of conservatives emerge.

Will Mitt Romney be too tired to fight the furious waves?
Or will we meekly have to wait and see
Or hope that a brighter day is coming
And it's just around the corner?

Thursday July 19, 2012

Mitt Romney

Come let us now resolve at last our differences!
I am different from other politicians,
But somehow appear to change my position on important
Issues readily, when the time is opportune.
For this I am unjustly scorned
Who wouldn't when the prize is the White House!

I lost, the first time I entered the race in 2008 and lost
My personal money.
I have never experienced poverty thanks to my father.
That I can't deny, but I maintained that status because
Of hard work as a small businessman.
For that I am also criticized, as phony
Because I am unable to understand the plight of the poor.

A rich man's time has come! I will tie the
Knot very soon! The time is short!
November will soon be here.
I am the only one that can beat President Obama.
Wasn't that what you want!
This would be the second fall of man!

Wednesday April 25, 2012

My Best Friend

Lord, I will praise you.
You have restored my integrity.
You have given new life to my efforts.
You have rescued me from deep waters.
You have blessed me time and time again.
You are a friend forever.

Wednesday July 19, 2012

On to the Breach

Fight on, President Obama.
God is on your side!
You can convert racism into
A gentle flame of love and hope
So that all Americans can benefit.
It is God's will!

Tuesday August 7, 2012

Presidential Nominee

There is Mitt Romney, former
Governor of Massachusetts and CEO
Bain Capital. He watched the market
And made a profit.
Managed failing and bankrupt businesses.
Turned them 'round to gold in foreign trade.
By outsourcing for cheaper wages in foreign countries
Now a billionaire by all accounts.
He saves his money in offshore banks
In the Cayman Islands, Switzerland, and the Dominican Republic.
To prevent paying Income Taxes in the USA
He spoke freely of his decision not to release
Any more than two years Income Tax returns.
He was a self-made man, and talked about
His success proudly, highlighting all the business
Deals he'd put through. So pompous is he, and
Very shrewd. No one guessed he really was in doubt.

Monday, September 10, 2012

Racism

Racism is a
Consuming fire
That will burn
All its supporters

Tuesday August 7, 2012

Romney Fest Up

Mitt Romney, Republican challenger for the Presidency
Is accused of flip-flopping on important issues.
I never really call myself pro-choice;
I will work and fight for stem cell research;
I saw my father march with Martin Luther King.
It's not possible to tell all!

Is this what wealth does to the wealthy?
Or is it only peculiar to the wealthy, who want to
Maintain themselves in the life style to which
They have become accustomed.

Romney acknowledged that he is different from his
Colleagues and other politicians because of his ability
To change his position on important issues, when the time is opportune.
Who wouldn't when the "White House" is the goal?
For this I am unjustly scorned by my colleagues and voters

Many call me a phony because I am unable to understand
The plight of the poor.
How can I? I have never been poor nor
Socialized with the poor. Everyone knows that!

I am severely criticized because I am rich.
I have never experienced poverty. Thanks to my father.
But I worked hard as a small businessman and
Governor to maintain my lifestyle.
I am proud of my Accomplishments.

A rich man's time has come! I will tie the
Knot very soon! The time is short!
November will soon be here. I am the only
Conservative who can beat President Obama.
Wasn't that what you wanted when you supported
Me for the Presidency!

May 16, 2012

The Time Has Come – 2

Being black in the United States of America,
Is a constant struggle. Black men are targeted
More than black women. Eloquence in a black man
Is regarded with disdain and contempt. Lack of
Fluency is received with humor and tolerance.

 A college education, especially at Harvard,
Princeton, or Columbia, is shrouded with
Skepticism and disrespect as is the case
Of President Obama, who is a graduate of
These institutions.

There is clamor recently, that President
Obama must produce his grades from these
Academic institutions in order to serve a second
Term as President of the United States of America.
This is the first demand of its kind in the history
Of the Presidency.

President Obama's qualifications as an academic
And politician is impeccable. The Nobel Peace
Prize awarded in 2010 is an indication of this.
Many of his countrymen thought the award was premature
And should not have been awarded to him.

The response of the American Society to the well read
Black man and those that are not is the same.
Both end up in a world of despair! In a job situation,
When the well-read apply for a job, he is rejected
Because he is overqualified, and the other, is
Rejected because he is underqualified.

If the United States of America is to regain her
Dominance in the World, she has to re-
Solve her economic problems and to end racism.

Refrain from using the word Negro, Hate Crime
Legislation, blocking Voter Registration, Redistricting
Constituencies, and cutting the Welfare Role
Will not suffice.

How long can America go to other countries
Touting Democracy and Freedom, when her citizens
Don't have Health Care, which is a right of Citizenship,
Don't have the right to vote in some states?
In states where they have the right to vote
They have restrictions that deny them the vote.

For black men and women in the United States of
America, freedom is a goal and not a reality.
Democracy is for the rich, and not for the poor.
In foreign countries, Democracy is encouraged in order to
Protect and sustain United States interest abroad
It's not for the natives of the country.
"United States of America, break up your fallow ground
And sow not among thorns."

Tuesday, August 23, 2012

True Love

True love is an enduring flame:
Always bright in sickness and in health;
Always ready to embrace his fellow man;
Always ready to be a Christian!

Tuesday, September 11, 2012

Veta E. Wilson

Born Kingston, Jamaica, West Indies
Received her RN and Midwifery Training in England and Scotland.
Degree in Health Science, Brooklyn College.
Bachelor of Science, Long Island University
Master of Science, Long Island University
Master of Public Health, Columbia University
Master of Divinity, New York Theological Seminary
In-service Instructor, New York City Correctional Health Service
Retired from New York City Correctional Health Service.

Wednesday, August 08, 2012

Victory Night

Sound the trumpet, beat the drums!
Here comes President Obama and his family.
Let them dance to any tune Bacchus sings.
Sweet is the pleasure after the pain.
The Obamas know it better than anyone.
They have routed all their foes.
They watched them fall one by one.
Only the victor wears the crown
Revenge! Revenge! The crowd cried.
There is no joy in revenge the Obamas responded
Let us all dance and sing with Bacchus and his par des.
"Victory is here at last," said the President.
"I will continue to fight until the gordian be gained."

Monday March 5, 2012

We must not forget

We must not forget his steadfast faith,
And true intent. Nor, when he first began.
The weary life he knew, and hours of travail
To perfect, The Affordable Care Act,
This was found constitutional by the Supreme Court
On June 28, 2012.

We must not forget the agony of waiting
For the Supreme Court to render judgment.
We must not forget that three years ago,
He was our hope for change.
We all then approved.
His steadfast faith never wavered.
We must not forget this!

Thursday, July 19, 2012

Whitney Houston

My heart skipped a beat, when I
Heard that Whitney Houston was
Found dead in a bathtub in her
Hotel room in California.

Poverty did not claim her!
God gave her a melodious and
Tender voice, that reaped a
Vast amount of money.
Yet, she fell prey to this age
Of drugs and revelry.

Over the years all the bloom and buoyancy
Of life fled. Leaving death: the common
End of classes rich and poor, to ride in
And end her misery!

What a loss to family and friends and to the world.
Who bolster and sustain her to the end.
Don't beat up on yourselves. Everyone did their best,
There must have been times when the burden
Became too heavy, and you longed for a respite
However brief!

 Now is the time for family
And friends and the world to grieve their
Irreparable loss. The end has come too soon!
God knows best He always does.

Sunday August 05, 2012

I Am Alpha and Omega

Crown me with roses and thorns while I am in office.
 Let's drink our wine and gall while I am there:
  Don't wait till I am gone.
After my departure, I nothing crave.
 History is kind to all Presidents,
  Because all are stoic in the grave.
"I am Alpha and Omega"; this is my legacy.

Monday 07/22/13

I Hear Different Tunes.

I hear different tunes: some more destructive, others disturbing.
Political pundits say racism will not be resolved in America.
The country is polarized.
Blacks are reconciled to the fact that they are no longer
The determining factor needed to ensure victory in the polls.
President Obama is more centrist in how he deals with racism.
The disturbing faction headed by Sen. Ted Cruz, Tea Party Conservative,
Ended his talkathon to dismantle President Obama's Affordable Care
Act after twenty-one hours and nineteen minutes.
No member of the Republican leadership came to Sen. Cruz's aid.
Sen. Ted Cruz wants to derail the Spending Bill to deny Democrats
The ability to strip and defund "Obama Care" provision out, a strategy
That put him at odds with Republicans who fear that the move would spark
A shutdown of government.
Sen. Ted Cruz called those who were unwilling to vote to stop
Obama Care are like Nazi appeasers.
At the White House meeting, convened by President Obama
With the Congress and the Senate, President Obama
Had the final tune, "I will not negotiate government delay
Of Obama Care."

October 4, 2013

Inauguration Day

In proud humility, I, Barak Obama,
Will take the Presidential Oath of Office
For the Second time.
I hope all Americans will repeat it with me,
Because it is your day.
You made it possible.
My wife, my children, and Mother-in-Law
Will share our lives with you for another four years.
We thank you for the opportunity, and
We thank God for making this day Possible

This is a historic occasion because I
Will be the Third Democratic President to
Serve two terms in Seventy-Five years.
What a privilege! This is the end of an era for
African Americans in the United States,
If the Republican Party has its way,
I will be the first and the last black Democratic President.

Pour out the wine without restraint.
Drink, drink to the last drop!
Forty-seven percent or one hundred percent
Of you, who cares! I hope when this
Anniversary comes around, African Americans
Will be glad that they celebrated.

However, we have a very difficult task before us
But I hope to work with Congress and the
Senate to put forward a comprehensive
Agenda to include Immigration Reform,
Gun Control, Economic and Foreign Policy

Reforms. Although we are outnumbered
We will continue to stride the blast
With confidence; It is my hope that we
Will have a better second term than the
First. In the years to come, you will
Remember this Inauguration day with
Pride. To God be the glory! Great things
He has done! God bless America.

Our Journey Is Not Complete
– Inauguration Pledge

Our journey is not:
Complete until our wives,
Our mothers and daughters
Can earn a living equal
To their efforts.

Our journey is not complete:
Until our gay brothers
And sisters are treated
Like anyone else under the law.

Our journey is not complete:
Until no citizen is forced to
Wait for hours to exercise
The right to vote.

Our journey is not complete:
Until we find a better way
To welcome the striving, hope-
Ful immigrants who still see
America as a land of opportunity.

Our journey is not complete
Until bright, young students
And engineers are enlisted in
Our workforce rather than expelled
From our country.

Our journey is not complete
Until all our children from the

Streets of Detroit to the Hills of
Appalachia to the quiet lanes
Of Newtown know that they
Are cared for and cherished
And always safe from harm.

Thursday, February 21, 2013

The Decline of the GOP

You have lost that vital spark that made
You rule. The political roost for many years
As the GOP rebounds from disastrous
Election Day loses and analyzes what it all means,
The party is criticized by is executives, its members
And the country as a whole.

The criticisms were brutal and divisive. The
Republican Party is becoming irrelevant.
Glenn Beck, Rush Limbaugh, Sean Hannity are to be blamed
For GOP's woes.
Republicans will not compromise.
"No" is not a policy!

To add insult to injury, Karl Rove, the Architect in
George W. Bush's presidency, and Dick Morris, former
Advisor to President Bill Clinton, were dismissed.
This rapid change dampen the spirit, draws
Many breaths away. It is feared this may be the end.
The death of the party. God forbid!

There is a massive change in the demographics and
Cultural diversity of party members. Bobby Jindal,
Governor of Louisiana, called on the party to re-
Calibrate the compass of conservatism. He
Further stated that the party does not need to change
Its values but "Might need to change just about
Everything else we do."

Is the massive change possible, when the
Tea Party faction with its leader, Sarah Palin

Is still inside. Some of the Tea Party congressmen
Lost their seat in the last election. Newcomers,
Ted Cruz of Texas is trying to establish himself
As an obstructionist, and is destined to bring back
The age of Senator Joseph McCarthy.

It is agreed that the party has to change its
Image and attract more women, Hispanics, and blacks.
The Clarion call within and outside the party
Is repent! Repent! Repent! If you don't, your days
Are numbered. Would this be a loss to the United
States of America, who knows?
Thursday, February 21, 2013

The Only Woman

Hillary Diane Rodham Clinton, is no stranger
To American Politics.
During the years, she has played many
Roles: Wife, Mother, Mother-in-law,
First Lady of the United States, First Lady
Of Arkansas, Senator, Lawyer, and Secretary
Of State for Foreign Affairs.

Unlike many women who had to juggle wife,
Motherhood, and professional responsibility,
We have never heard her groan under any of
These responsibilities. Her daughter, whom she
Raised, is a well-mannered young lady. All of
America is proud of her.
She has her share of marital and political problems
But she has handled them with wisdom, decorum, and finesse.

Now she has retired to take a
Respite from all her responsibilities
And to make a decision about her
Future, we hope her decision is to be
The first woman President of the
United States of America.
She is the only woman in USA
Qualified to do so. She is
A politician, all the choices that
She has made in her professional
Life qualifies her to fill that role.
I hope I live to see her run.
Run, Hillary, run. All of America
Is behind you.

Thursday, February 21, 2013

The Presidential Race

Run, Barack Obama, Run!
Mitt Romney can't catch you.
Romney's only talent is making money
For himself and the rich.
Barack, yours is a nobler reason for running.
You want to improve the plight of the poor.
God will plea the cause of the poor.
Run, Barack, run, Romney can't catch up with you.
Run hard, run strong, the whole country is behind you.
Barack Obama, you have won! You have won!
You have won a second term as President of the
United States.

Wednesday, January 30, 2013

The Slaughter of the Innocent

Weep with me, all you that hear of this tragedy;
Twenty children and six adults lost their lives,
In Sandy Hook Elementary School, Newtown, Connecticut,
On Friday, December 14th, 2012.

All of the children were first-graders, eight boys and twelve
Girls ages six or seven years old. School personnel, all women:
The Principal, Psychologist, and teachers.
This was the worse gun tragedy in America to date.

Oh, what a day when fate turns cruel!
Nancy Lanza, a fifty-two-year-old old divorcee, mother of two sons,
And a gun enthusiast, with an arsenal of five guns.
Two powerful handguns, two traditional hunting rifles,
And a semi-automatic rifle. All were legally acquired
And were registered. Nancy often took her sons to the
Shooting ranges in the suburbs of Northeast New York State.

Tom Lanza, twenty years old, lived with his mother. He had a
Developmental disorder which made his socialization and
Management difficult for a single parent. It is not known
What triggered this rampage of violence. Tom Lanza
Shot and killed his mother as she slept in her bed. Then
Like a dazed sleepwalker he went to the School and
Gunned down the children, their teachers, administrators,
Then himself.

Twenty-eight persons lost their lives in this massacre.
Death is a cruel thing because it can't demand
Justice for its victims. But those of us who are left
Behind can cooperate with the Vice President, Joe Biden,

Who was commissioned by President Barack Obama
To head a task force that will provide the President
With Gun Control Legislative recommendations.
If it succeeds, then we all can say death is swallowed up in Victory!
America wanted to do something about the problem
Of Gun Violence—Now is the time.

Friday, January 04, 2013

Backlash from the Tea Party Movement.

All over the United States of America, men women and children
Are starving because of unavoidable economic circumstances.
The whole country is experiencing the worst economic collapse.
In thirty years. Workers are laid off in the private sector as well as Government.
     Many people who regarded themselves as "working class,"
No longer regard themselves as such, because they are not working.
Changes are apparent in the life style of the "middle class,"
Because economic recovery is slow many have lost their homes:
Due to high mortgage rates and foreclosures.
     As a result, the "working class" and the "middle class"
Are questioning these terms because of their economic reality.
The dreaded term "lower class" this was considered insulting
Is on the rise. Also on the rise is the disparity between the rich and the poor.
While the income of the rich is expanding the income of the poor
Is declining.
     One does not hear much about the "upper class," because
They are perceived as the ones who benefit from the current
Financial crisis, which caused reduction in salaries and wages of workers.
Cut in benefits and working hours; jobs outsourced to countries
Where labor is cheap; factories are sent abroad; workers
Became redundant; and the numbers of unemployed increased.

     The Private sector felt that the Affordable Care Act would
Increase their health care cost and reduce their profits.
In order to reduce cost, they decided to reduce the workforce.
Some refused to pay health care benefits; some no longer
Provide Health Care for their employees, and others reduced
Employees working hours.
     As a result, members of Congress who were supported
By the "Tea Party" movement, within the Republican Party,
Decided to defund the Affordable Care Act.
Although the Act was judged legal by the Supreme Court,
The House of Representatives is controlled by the Republicans.

Who want to defund the Affordable Care Act and who have
Since President Obama's election, tried to deny any
Legislative achievements by stubborn, uncooperative maneuvers
Designed to block President Obama's policies for the last
Six years.
      There is much antagonism to the Affordable Care Act,
Which is designed to improve the health of all Americans,
And ensures a healthy workforce who can compete with
Other industrial Nations. Yet, many Southern States
Have rejected the Medicaid Expansion.
Senators and House of Representative men and women
May flourish or fade at the will of their constituents.

What America needs if she is to maintain dominance
In the world is a healthy, skilled workforce that can compete
With other workers from other countries. Strong Labor
Unions, to bargain for a living wage scale for workers,
Good working condition in factories. Safe working environments
A strong Middle class, Strong working class. The country
Must have pride in its workforce. When these things are destroyed
They can never be supplied.
Support President Obama, America!
He is on the right tract.

Saturday January 04, 2014

He didn't lie to us knowingly

No one likes to be told a lie! I am no different
    But I know that President Barack Obama
Would not lie to the American people deliberately.
    He chose a career of service, although he was educated
And he could get a lucrative job.

He had a vision for his country and its people
    And the will to execute it.
He took a job as a community organizer in a Chicago project
    So that he could get first-hand information of the struggle
That poor people have to undergo daily. Some people's
    Situations change daily; others may not.

President Obama knows that the United States of America
    Is divided racially and politically.
So when he went to organize the people in the project
    He did not foist his opinion on them.
Instead, he worked with them to empower them to act
    To change their circumstance. Once they recognize
The need for change they will organize themselves
    And seek the change they need.

Armed with that knowledge, he decided to go into politics big time!
    He became a Congressman, a Senator, and then the President.
President Obama's detractors don't know what they are talking about.
    Where were they, when President Obama laid the foundation of Trust?
Between himself and the American people. President Obama
    Is a man of integrity. He would not knowingly mislead the American people.

When President Bill Clinton asked President Barack Obama
To apologize to the American people,
President Bill Clinton knew that President Obama
Did not intend to mislead the American people.

President Bill Clinton made the request out of his own self-interest:
He thinks his wife, Hillary Clinton, may run for the Presidency in 2016.

President Barack Obama compiled with the request,
But he paid a bitter price for doing so: His rating dropped.
The apology to the nation became a football to opponents.
His attitude when he faced the nation was aloft and resolute
And seem to imply: No other balm will I give!

The President will see that the computers are fixed
So that the enrollment can be completed; it would appear
That thing are under control now because the President
Has moved on.

The Republicans want to destroy your legacy. Let them go ahead.
You have weathered every storm, the prize you
Sought is won. They can't destroy the Affordable Care Act.
It is here to stay. You will be the first and last
Black President for centuries to come. You deserve it.

January 21, 2014

Nelson Mandela

July 18, 1918 – Dec. 5, 2013

A light from our world is gone,
A voice that we love is still, a beacon
    Of hope is gone to rest forever.
He will be remembered as long as the
    Struggle for freedom exists because,
He showed courage and lack of ranker
    Towards his captors after being
Imprisoned for twenty-seven years
    On notorious Robben Island for fighting
        Apartheid in his country, South Africa.

January 21, 2014

Racism A Reluctant Topic

I have always wondered why President Obama never discusses Racism.
When most of his legislative problems and the disrespect shown to him,
And his family is a direct result of their color.

To discuss the problem would give his supporters some hope,
That this canker that ravaged the country for so many years,
Must be removed root and branch if the economy is to recover
And the United States of America regain her place in the world economy.

Black people are citizens of the United States; as a result
The Government has a responsibility to its Black Citizens as well
As White Citizens and this responsibility is recognized by
The Constitution of the United States of America, which states,
"All men are created equal and endowed with life, liberty and the
Pursuit of happiness."

What caused the President to break his silence and speak out now?
This is all conjecture: As a Law Professor, he was astonished
At the outcome of David Zimmerman's trial.
Zimmerman was given the gun he used to Kill Trayvon Martin,
His shackles were removed and he was pronounced free from
All responsibilities for Trayvon Martin's death.
The President's astonishment provoked a sense of pain in him,
That we have never seen during his presidency.
The President of the United States of America was deeply moved,
And fought back tears as he reflected that Trayvon Martin could
Be his son; Trayvon Martin was black like him, while White America
Was Jubilant, on many television networks celebrating
The triumph of the "Stand Your Ground Law."

The President was severely criticized by many
News outlets. Despite the reaction to the Verdict,
The President and his wife reaffirm their
Commitment to fight for Health Care and equal
Justice for all Americans.

Thursday, January 02, 2014

The End of My Two Terms

Michelle, Shasha, and Malia, I have completed my two terms
As President of the United States of America.
I have weathered every storm; the prize I sought is won.
Let's sing and shout, thank God we have survived!

I can hear the church bell ringing, can you?
The people are jubilant; I can hear them cry—Never again!
"The White House" will be "White" again, but will it?
God forbid! I left the "White House" safe and sound, better than I got it.

My voyage is completed; the Victor must check the objects won.
The Affordable Care Act has been battered but showed resilience.
And so did we! The Nation watched but the detractors
Never once cried, "Compromise." They would prefer to kill the
Thing they knew will give the poor relief than touch the one percent.

Oh, America, I love you with a love that increases every day,
But wonder what the future holds for you,
When you cling tenaciously to the past.
We must break up the fallow ground of hatred and mistrust.
Slavery was abolished one hundred fifty years ago.

We are a free people: We are Americans,
Together we must build an edifice of hope and love:
In which all peoples can live and raise a family.
And build a nation, of which we all can be proud,
My family and I will strive to meet that goal.

Thursday January 02, 2014

A Week of Victories

Lord, help me accept my last term in office
With the same hope I had when I became President
Help me set the best example should others
Choose to follow me.
Lord, when I'm feeling overwhelmed; let me focus
On my family, keep on believing, keep on trying,
And keep on going.

I have preached compromise to my colleagues
From my first term in office. The reason being,
I am President of the United States of America,
And Commander-in-Chief of the Armed Forces.
But I am not head of the Democratic Party.
The House Democratic Leader currently is Nancy Pelosi.
The Senate Democratic Leader currently is Harry Reid.
The Democratic Party is ruled and controlled by
The Democratic National Committee whose current head
Is Debbie Wasserman Schultz who assists
The President pursuing his agenda and
Getting Democratic Candidates elected.
Joseph Biden is Vice President and Chairman of the Senate.
I am the first black man to be President of
The United States of America.
Lord, help me to accept the joys of ambition
Without arrogance of regrets.
I thank God for my mother, my father, grandparents,
Sister, my wife and children, mother-in-law, bother-in-law,
Vice President Joseph Biden and his family, who have
Contributed to the success of this remarkable journey.

I know there is a brighter day coming for me when,
I will sit back and count the victories I have won.

Among them is "Same Sex Marriage is Legal Nationwide."
Not only because it was a campaign promise, but "I
Feel when all Americans are treated as equal
We are all freer."
Then there is my signature achievement, "The Affordable Care Act"
Called "Obama Care."
I will work with the Governors who did not accept
"Medicaid Expansion" for their States
Because I would like everyone to get Universal Healthcare coverage.

July 19, 2015

Early Reflection on My Presidency

Lord, help me accept my last term in Office
With the same hope I had when I became President.
Help me to set the best examples should others
Choose to follow me.
Lord, when I'm feeling overwhelmed, let me focus on my
Family, keep on believing, keep on trying, and keep on going.

I have preached compromise to my colleagues
From my first term in office. The reason being,
I am President of the United States of America,
And Commander-in-Chief of the Armed Forces.
But I am not head of the Democratic Party.

The House Democratic Leader is Nancy Pelosi.
The Senate Democratic Leader is Harry Reid.
The Democratic Party is ruled and controlled by the
Democratic National Committee, whose head is
Debbie Wasserman Schultz who assists the President
Pursuing his agenda and getting Democratic
Candidates elected to Congress. Joe Biden is Vice President
And Chairman of the Senate.
I am the first Negro to be President of the United
States of America. Lord, help to accept the joys
Of ambition without arrogance or regrets.
I thank God for my mother, father, and my grandparents,
My sister, my wife and children, my Vice President,
Joe Biden and his family who have contributed
To this remarkable journey.
I knew there is a brighter day coming for me
When I will sit back and count the victories I have won.
And first among them will be the Supreme Court
Ruling on the Affordable Care Act June 25th, 2015

June 26th, 2015

Hilary Clinton for President

Is Hilary Clinton ready to be President of the United States?
Yes, because she is able.
Will Hilary Clinton run for the Presidency in 2016?
Yes, because she is able.
Will she make mincemeat of her opponents?
Yes, because she is able.
Hilary has found a new institution
With her daughter, Chelsea, and her husband, Bill.
Yes, because she is able.
This promises to be a formidable venture,
Equipped to meet the challenges of this century
Politics in America with all the changes in demographics.
Yes, because she is able.
Run, Hilary, the whole country and the world are behind you
But your enemies do not wish you well!
There is a saying, "Dog wag him tail fi suit him size and match his stamina"
But we have till 2016.
So, watch it!
There is many a slip between the cup and the lip!

08/17/2015

Political Dog Fight

President Obama, I heard your speech
In defense of your position on the TPP.
All the Trade Unions banded together with the Democrats
To Defend workers right to a living wage and,
Keeping jobs in the United States of America.

President Obama, you were critical of Senator
Elizabeth Warren, who does not support the TPP,
Because she feels that it is in the interest of manufacturers.
Workers are against it, because outsourcing jobs to
Foreign countries is not in their best economic interest.
The vote on this issue in Congress resulted in
Defeat of the President and the solidarity of the Democrats.

Senator Elizabeth Warren insists that President Obama
Should write his vision and make it plain on paper
That Legislators and constituents can see it and make up
Their minds if it is in their best interest.
The President's vision in time will speak and will not lie
If it is good.
Thank you, Senator Elizabeth Warren, for
Your Defense of the working class.

07/23/2015

Violence in the United States of America

There are many attitudes to violence in the United States of America.
Some feel that violence is a justifiable response to provocation,
And Human Nature, while people in the Entertainment Industry
See it as a suitable form of entertainment.

The Mental Health Community state that big factors are Stress
And Depression, treatment would include counseling, medication,
Electroconvulsive Therapy, to ensure and maintain mental stability.

There are a group of white people who see violence as a cleansing agent
And use it to get rid of black people; such a person is Dylan Roof,
A white twenty-five years old member of the Klu Klux Clan who gunned down
Nine church members in the Emanuel AME Church in Charleston,
South Carolina, on June 17, 2015. Roof entered the church and sat
Quietly for an hour in Bible Study, then pulled out a .45 caliber
Handgun and shot the victims at close range, killing nine people.

This cowardly act killed the pastor of the Church, Clementa Carlos Pinckney,
Who was also a Senator for forty-one years. He was eulogized
By Barack Obama, President of the United States of America.
Also present at the ceremony was Joseph Biden,
Vice President of the United States of America.

This incident reignited a national debate on gun control,
Removal of the Confederate Flag from Government Buildings,
Because it is the symbol of White supremacy.

Racism, because survivors told police that Roof told them
He came to the church "to kill black people."
All over the country there is a cry for justice
Roof was charged with nine counts of murder
And three counts of attempted murder.
Roof is awaiting trial.

July 19, 2015

Wat a Courageous Woman

Mi no understand di black and white Business
Dem call racism.
For wha day mi prove it wid Rachel Dolezal.
She come pon di television cryin she lost her job,
As a NAACP Executive, because she identify as black.
Mi thought dem would be glad dat a limey white woman
A call herself a spade.
But di whole country tun upside down.

Dolezal seh she felt limited to her Biological identity.
Lawd, listen to mi, mi never see such braveness so.
Di head man at di NAACP say dat white people
Are welcome to join di organization as long as dey
Carry out di goals of di organization.
Some blacks never like his explanation.

Mi know Rachel well, she have a good heart
Better than some born black people.
All mi can seh, gal shed yuh tears!
Everything is a nine days talk.
Thank God you no under dat deh strain now.

Things so bad dat nowadays pickney a tell dem
Parents what sex dem want to be.
So mi seh to mi self mi nuh see what di
Big deal is if she seh she wants to be a spade
Instead of a limey.

08/17/2015

White House Briefing

Listen to mi, President Obama
Stan up pon U dignity.
Don't allow nobady
Fi teck libaty wid U.
Let dem know U a di
President of di United States of America.

What a crosses!
Di man say him a journalist.
And stan up in a briefin room
Wid all di newspaper people,
Secret Service Agents, and guests
And want to disrespect di President.

A glad U put him in a him place
Stand up pon U dignity.
U are di Commander-in-chief
Of di Armed Forces of di United States of America

Don't allow no white man fi tek liberty wid U
Because U is no ordinary black man.
U is di first black President of di United States of America
To how tings go, you may be di first and di last!

July 19, 2015